When

is Sick

a child's guide to learning that
someone they love has cancer

by Lisa Burns

This book is dedicated to:
Stephen (my handsome man)
Brooke
Emily
Heather
Jacob
Jay
Kayla
Leanne
my Poppy

Dr. Nabell, Dr. Pressey, Dr Woodworth
& all the nurses & medical staff who treated my husband

All those who have courageously fought cancer
& those who have lovingly walked alongside them

ISBN: 978-0-578-88692-3

The pages you'll be reading
come from experience and thought
As my husband battled cancer
and the lessons we've been taught.

Come, let's snuggle with this book.
Let's sit down and let's share
How we'll best support our _____
and show them that we care.

Let's start with the basics.
Let's talk about what's wrong:
Cancer started growing
where it just doesn't belong.

"Why?" you may be wondering,
or maybe even "How?"
I wish I had the answers
to those very questions now.

When we cannot find the answers
we can trust God in our fears.
He knows each single "how" & "why"
that come with all our tears.

Will the days ahead be easy?
Some yes, while often no.
But faith and trust in God above
will help us as we go.

Praise God we're not alone
and He continues to provide.
He graciously gives us knowledge
and doctors who can guide.

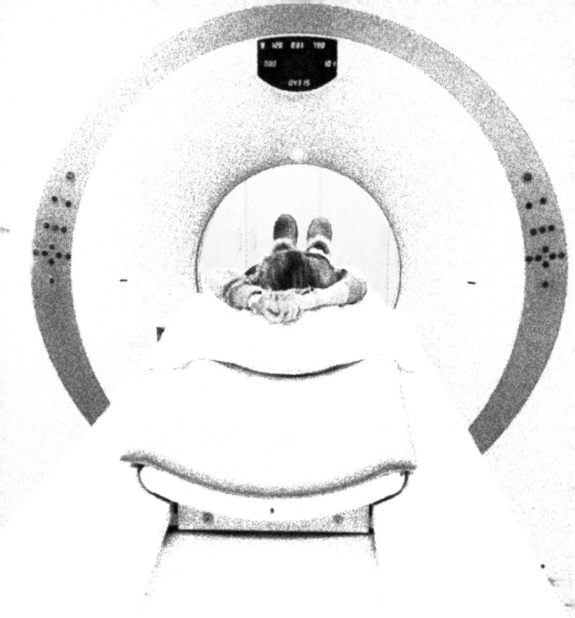

There are many types of treatments doctors use to try and cure. Let's talk about some options that our _____ may endure.

When doctors use strong medicine
to help cancer go away,
They call it "chemotherapy,"
or "chemo" as some say.

CHEMOTHERAPY

It can make _____ feel tired
and sleepy as can be.
Their tummy may become upset
and food can taste yucky.

Some chemos, but not all,
can make people lose their hair.
But even though their hair is gone,
their smile is still there!

With radiation doctors use
these very strong machines.
They aim them at the bad cells
and shoot special laser beams.

Like chemo, radiation, too,
can make them want to rest.
Let's snuggle and stay quiet
to help _____ feel their best.

Sometimes cancer's found
in just a single spot or two
And surgery may be the best
and safest choice to do.

There are many other options
to help cancer go away.
It all depends upon the type
and where it is today.

Now that we've had a *lesson*
on what the *docs* can do,
Let's try and think what *we* can do
to *help us* all get through.

_____ is always there for you
so now it is your turn
To show them just how much you care
and all that you have learned.

How can you be a *helper*
when yet you're *not quite* grown?
You can be there for your _____
so they don't feel all *alone*.

One *easy* way to help them
is to simply *wash your hands.*
If friends are sick, *stay home* for now,
I'm *sure* they'll understand.

Germs can be real *scary*
when their body's *weak* to fight.
We want to keep those colds *away*
so _____ is alright.

Encourage _____ to take a walk
or just get up and move.
They may move slower than before
but soon they shall improve.

At times they may just want to nap
- be quiet as can be!
You can snuggle as you read a book
or both watch some tv.

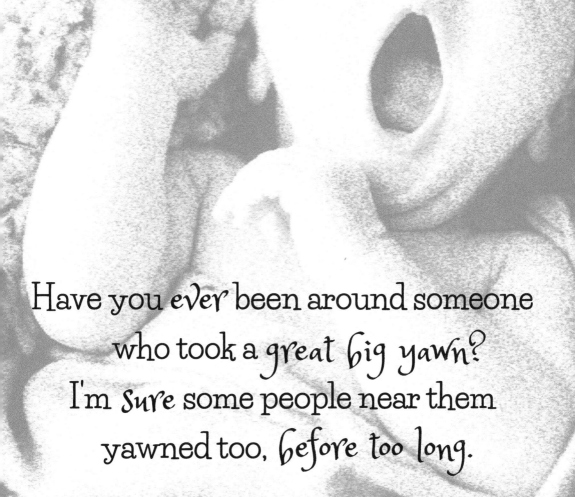

Have you *ever* been around someone
who took a *great big yawn?*
I'm *sure* some people near them
yawned too, *before too long.*

Do you know what's more contagious
than that simple breath of air?
A smile spreads more quickly
and lets _____ see you care.

If we smile around our _____
they may start to *smile too*,
Despite their *yucky* feelings
and *all* that they've been through.

On days when _____ feels their best
do something extra fun!
Create a new fun memory
before the day is done.

For these days may not be easy
and at times you will feel sad.
Years ahead choose to remember
all the good times that you had.

This time can be used for growing
closer to our Lord above.
A time to focus less on the pain
and more on His goodness & love.

This time can be used to *show others* that *despite* our sadness and pain, *God* creates beauty in suffering, like *flowers* after the rain.

This time can be used to
make memories
so when you look back
you'll recall

The happy times over the sad ones,
the redemption over the fall.

This time can be used to truly see
that God is so very near.
He lovingly walks alongside us
and counts each single tear.

This time can be used to grow our trust,
knowing God is in control,
And believing He's good no matter how
our lives may unfold.

This time can be *purposeful*
in seeing good *during* the pain,
Knowing that *even* in hard times
sweet memories can remain.

Let's choose to *focus* on the good
despite all we're going through.
Let's *treasure* these extra memories
_____ gets to make with you!

Throughout the following pages,
let's write down and recall
Our joyful times and moments,
as the Lord works through it all.

Glossary

Cells

Cells are the "building blocks" of our human body.
Cells are responsible for carrying out all of our body's functions.

Cancer

Cancer is a disease that happens when cells *that are not normal* grow & spread.
Normal body cells grow and divide and know when to stop. Over time, these
normal cells die. Cancer cells, on the other hand, uncontrollably grow & divide,
and then they don't die when they're supposed to; this can make a person sick.

Chemotherapy

Chemotherapy is the name for medicine that is used to treat and cure cancer.
There are many different types of chemotherapy treatments; some are given in
the hospital through an IV, while others are taken at home through pills.

Radiation

Radiation therapy is high energy therapy that is used to treat and cure cancer.
Radiation can either be internal (inside the body) or external (outside the body).
With external radiation, doctors use large machines to carefully
aim the right amount of radiation at cancerous tumors.
With internal radiation, the radioactive agent goes into the patient's body
by injection (like a shot) or ingestion (swallowing).

Tumor

A tumor is a cluster, or group, of cells. Not all tumors are cancerous.
A growing, cancerous tumor can hurt the healthy cells around it.

Surgery

Surgery, sometimes called an operation, is when doctors fix
something inside a person's body to make that person feel better.
Doctors usually remove or help fix the problem area by using special tools.
Don't worry - the patient will be asleep and will not feel any pain during surgery.

Hope

Hope is the confident, joyful expectation that God is working,
both now and in the future, for my good and His glory.

Faith

Faith is the assurance of things hoped for, the conviction of things not seen.

Hebrews 11:1

A note from the author...

Each cancer journey is different.
This book is simply some takeaways I learned, first hand, as my husband endured 29 rounds of chemo, 12 weeks of radiation, multiple surgeries and hospital stays, and several relapses, all while raising our two young boys. I know the days feel so very long, but try and cling to the good in each day. Choose to find something to be thankful for.

"Do not be anxious about anything, but in everything by prayer and supplication with thanksgiving let your requests be made known to God. And the peace of God, which surpasses all understanding, will guard your hearts and your minds in Christ Jesus." Philippians 4:4-8
Remind yourself of who God is - His character, His love, His goodness - which never changes, despite our circumstances.

Some practical tips for the caretaker:
Document everything! This recommendation came from one of my dearest friends, Beth, who walked through cancer with her husband a few years before we did. Throughout each day of chemo (and at least a week following), I documented what medicines my husband took & when, what he ate & when, and summarized how he felt; this was an incredibly helpful reference during each subsequent round of chemo. Looking back at our records helped calm fears, reminded us to take certain meds longer, and allowed us to see trends, such as when he would start to feel better, which enabled us to plan something fun and memorable as a family.

Our boys don't remember the stress of moving to Houston for 2 months (during the holidays!)	They remember the fun adventure we took & the memories we made in our "new home town".
Our boys don't remember the fear of seeing "different" looking people at the hospital.	They remember Mr. Gary, the cool man in the wheelchair, who talked to them through his throat box.
Our boys don't remember Daddy feeling awful at chemo.	They remember fun Nurse Kevin & Barbara, who always gave them M&Ms.
Our boys don't remember that Daddy was too sick to wake up early on Christmas morning.	They remember sitting on the floor of the apartment kitchen (so they wouldn't see the Christmas presents), making monkey bread as we waited.
Our boys don't remember the fears associated with radiation.	They remember the excitement of buckling daddy down to the table, the puzzles we made as we waited, & the friends we made in the waiting room.
Our boys don't remember that Mommy was too exhausted to cook.	They remember the body of Christ in action, lovingly bringing us meals.

They remember the moments of joy.
Praise the Lord. Lisa

Lightning Source UK Ltd.
Milton Keynes UK
UKHW051916090421
381726UK00003B/116